A Promise to Great Grandmother

Cycle to Norway

George R. Benson

Copyright © 2023 George R. Benson. All rights reserved.
Published by George R. Benson
ISBN 978-1-4467-6666-8

This book is dedicated to all who have dreams and goals and seek courage to live them.

Table of Contents

Introduction	5
Decision Made	7
Eyes Wide Open	19
Horrible Timing for a Pit Stop	21
First Kilometres in Europe	24
Discovery of the Friendly and Beautiful Dutch	28
Bike Problems Begin	34
A Belgian Wife?	38
Strength Grows	44
Discovery of French Attitude	49
Disadvantages of Camping in the Wild	60
A Long Walk Home	64
A Language Misunderstanding	69
Introduction to Italian Forwardness	71
A Long Interruption to Joy	74
A Turn for the Better	83
The Leaning Tower of Pisa	86
The Analogy of a Sculpture	89

A Symphony of Flashing Lights	93
A Summit Surprise	97
A Winter Dream Job	103
A Needed Rest	109
Into the Wind and Out of the Barn	113
No Bananas	119
Germany and Denmark	122
Missed Ferry	124
The Miracle	130
Fei Deg!	138
Unwanted Hugs	144
A True Viking	149
The Last Leg	153
The Completion of My Promise	158
A Moment of Fame	164
Closing	168
Afterward	173
Back Home	183
George with Great Grandmother	186

Introduction

In 1988, at the age of 27, in the days before cell phones, the internet, social media and global positioning systems, George set off to Europe with his bicycle and a one way ticket on a solo journey to fulfil a promise he made as a boy to his Norwegian great grandmother. In four months he cycled, unsupported, over 8,000 kilometres (5,000 miles) through nine countries to not only fulfil his promise, but to also develop his confidence to have dreams and goals and to live them. He ended up staying in Europe for a year, working at various jobs in Norway, the Netherlands, and Austria.

Due to the fact that near the beginning of his bike tour, George needed to drop weight to slow down the process of bike spokes breaking, most of the images in this book are from a variety of sources. He began the tour with his father's 1980's style heavy

Minolta camera. Early on in his journey, the camera was one of many pieces of equipment he left with a farmer in the Netherlands. In retrospect, not having a camera and not having to stop to take pictures all the time, George more fully lived in the moment. Some of the images are George's own, others are from fellow travellers who sent photos to his parents in Oregon, and the rest are images of postcards he collected on his journey.

Decision Made

    It shouldn't take a near death experience to get someone to live their dream, but for me, it did. Douglas Fir tree branches crunched and Ford Taurus headlights beamed into the dark thick forest when I woke. Full size trees came into view as my car sped, crashing through the forest. I remembered I had been nodding off, fighting sleep, as I wound my way up the road to Skykomish, Washington and my ski lift operator apartment in a mountain lodge. My arms straightened at the steering wheel and my stomach tensed as I realised this may be the last seconds of my life. Branches continued to crash against my car and massive trees swept by on my left and right. I was sure one tree would soon be directly in front of me waiting for a smashing head on collision and the start of excruciating pain and probably the end of my life.

    Suddenly, my car came to a stop without a head on smash. Something had caused me to stop without a violent end. On the radio the song "He's got the whole world in his hands" played. I remembered I had turned the station to soothing music that I thought would help me stay awake. I took stock of my situation. Was I alright? All I noticed was my seatbelt had held my chest tight. There was little, if no pain. I looked left and right and saw the bark of large Douglas Fir trees. Instead of going head on into a tree, I had wedged in between two trees. They held me tight. I looked out my window and saw the Skykomish river below. The trees had saved me from flying off a 20 foot (6 meter) high bank into the river.

    That's it, I thought, I'm going. No more waffling about whether or not I was going to Europe to start my solo bike tour. I'm alive. I'm given another chance at life. I opened my sunroof and climbed out the top. I climbed a steep bank back to the main road and walked in the dark along the road. The doubt of my ability to follow through on a boyhood promise vanished. I was steeled in determination to follow through with my plans. I felt born again. I waved down a truck driver who stopped and gave me a ride up to Skykomish and the beginning of my final preparations to depart for Amsterdam.

    The promise was made on the lap of my Norwegian great grandmother when I was a young boy. Great grandmother Nelsina left western Norway at the age of 19 in 1906 to join her sister working at a hotel in San Francisco in the post gold-rush boom. She never returned to Norway. As a matter of fact, she never made it to San Francisco. She met a Norwegian farmer on the boat to Ellis Island, Ole Olson, got married and eventually settled in a remote area of Montana near Helena. There she had three children, including my grandmother Olivia. After her husband died, she moved to Coronado, California with her three children, where her sister had moved.

    As a young boy in Coronado, California, I often sat on her lap and loved to hear her speak Norwegian with my grandmother. I often asked her if she would like to go back to Norway and she said she would love to but was too old to return. I promised her I would go to Norway for her and that I would ride my bike there. As a boy in Coronado, I constantly rode my Schwinn purple bike around the numerous street blocks and along the golf course in Coronado looking for stray golf balls. If I could do this, I was sure I could ride to Norway.

    The promise never left my thoughts and aspirations through my high school and university years. After high school I didn't want to go to university because I wanted to live out my promise to my great grandmother. After university, I didn't want to start a career or commit to a long term relationship until I lived my promise, which had become my dream. Deep in my heart I knew I had to ride my bike to Norway and to the home of my great grandmother before I could make major life commitments. In my soul, I knew that living this dream would change me also.

I had trouble finding the courage to follow through on my promise. My two older brothers and two older sisters had all married soon after graduating from university and each stepped into career type jobs. My father was a former Navy lieutenant and school administrator and expected us, especially us boys, to live a traditional life. When I mentioned my desire to follow my dream and promise to bike to Norway he told me that people who do such things usually end up with no direction in life.

I loved my Dad and Mom and wanted to please them. After graduating from

Whitworth University in Spokane, Washington in May of 1984, I moved back in with my parents in Lake Oswego, Oregon and I went through the motions of looking for a career job. I eventually took a bank manager training job.

After two weeks of restless sleep knowing that I wasn't being true to myself, I packed up my Toyota pick-up truck in the middle of the night and left my parents and their home in the morning. It was a shock to them and me, but I knew that if I was going to be myself and live my dreams, I had to go out on my own.

I spent the next two years trying different jobs that included driving a bus for a weight loss camp in San Diego and working as a salesman at a sporting goods store in Denver, Colorado. I was thinking of saving money for my Norwegian promise and also tried to please a college girlfriend who was still finishing up her degree in Spokane. She said she only wanted to be with me if I could demonstrate an ability to have a career type job. That relationship didn't last.

I ended up in Seattle, Washington as a sales representative for a paper distribution company, again going through the motions of trying to have a career type job for which my parents and my then new girlfriend would be proud.

After a year and a half with the company the sales manager called me to come into the main office. I had a feeling there was some type of promotion coming, meaning a bigger commitment to the company. At the age of 26, the conflict between the desires of others and my desires came to a peak. I walked into the meeting with the sales manager and told him I wanted to leave the company because I had some unfinished personal business. This shocked him and my girlfriend. They couldn't believe I would walk away from the opportunity to make even more money and to start a family.

At the age of 26 I decided to take the first real steps to live my promise to my great grandmother. I left my job and my girlfriend and moved to Skykomish, Washington to work as a lift operator at Stevens Pass ski resort. My plan was to live as simply as possible, work as many lift operator shifts as possible, and save money for my bike tour to Norway.

This was the change that not only started me in the direction of my Norwegian promise, but also moved me closer to discovering and being myself. I grew out my beard and let my hair grow long. I chopped up my suits and ties on the wood cutting block outside the lodge where I rented a room and started to hang out with people who had dreams of adventures like mine. I finally had people encouraging me to live my promise and dream.

In the months and days leading up to my departure for my flight to Europe with my bike, I was filled with excitement and doubt.

I was excited to buy my bike, an Italian Bianchi touring bike, panniers (which are the bags that hang on the bike to carry gear) and other touring equipment. It was exciting to look at a map of Europe and plan my route through ten countries and hope that after five months I would end up in western Norway. It was exciting to change my dollars into the money I would need for each country. At that time, the Euro was not known. Each country had its own currency. I ordered about 50 dollars from a Seattle bank for each of the ten countries I would be cycling through. This would be my starting money in each country.

    I also battled with great feelings of doubt that I could follow through on living this promise and dream all by myself. In my daily journal I often wrote how I didn't think I had the power to follow through on my plan. Occasional visits from my former girlfriend to my mountain home didn't help strengthen my courage either. At times I almost gave up my dream that winter of 1987-88 and nearly promised her I would stay and start a family.

In fact, my fateful near death car crash happened after driving down to Seattle to meet my former girlfriend for a pizza. The pizza date turned into a fight over why I left my sales job and her to go work as a lift operator at a ski resort.

I drove away in a daze and without confidence I would ever live my promise and dream. I was so close to living my dream, but maybe my former girlfriend and my dad were right. I was throwing away my life. About midnight, feeling tired and confused, I began the hour drive back to my mountain home and the near death accident.

Winter 1987-88
George at his lift operator job at Stevens Pass near Seattle.

George in Skykomish at the mountain lodge with his Ford Taurus after the crash.

Eyes Wide Open

On May 8, 1988 I could not believe I was stepping, alone, with a one way ticket, on a KLM flight from Seattle to Amsterdam with just my Bianchi touring bike and my touring gear. When the doors closed on the plane and we were airborne I was like a bird set free from a cage and a caterpillar escaping from the cocoon to become a butterfly.

I could not believe I was living my promise and dream! Once the seat belt lights were off I couldn't sit still. I walked up and down the isles with excitement and spent the hours looking out the small round windows near the flight attendants, marvelling at the snow fields over Canada and Greenland.

All my doubts disappeared. There was no turning back. I was beginning my promise to my great grandmother to ride to Norway for her. I had never felt so alive. My plan was to start in Amsterdam and cycle south through Belgium, France, Spain, and Italy before heading north toward Norway.

Horrible Timing for a Pit Stop

I stand in front of the main train station in Amsterdam. My bike and gear are in a cardboard bike box at my side. Tourists and locals hurry in every direction. I feel like I'm in a dream. I think, "Am I really here in Europe? Can this really be?" I am at the start of the dream and promise I started nearly 20 years ago.

I feel like jumping up and down and hooting and hollering out of excitement. I want to start assembling my bike to start my tour, but realise I have a more pressing need. I need to go to the toilet. What should I do? Carry my bike box and gear around with me looking for a toilet? No. I decide to reach out to a passerby. I ask a middle aged woman passing by if she can help me. She is a Dutch woman with a friendly smile and hello. She tells me she is happy to wait with my bike as I go to the toilet.

I search for a toilet and finally find one. It is a pay toilet and I don't have a Guilder coin. This was a time before the present Euro. I do have some Dutch Guilders in notes and go searching for someone who will give me some change. I worry about my bike thinking about how horrible it would be to lose my bike before my tour even began.

I finally get some coins and come back to the toilet only to find a line has formed. Not only am I desperate to use the toilet, but I'm also feeling panicked that the woman will have run out of patience waiting for me to return. It has been ten minutes since I left her.

After another five minutes, I'm finally able to use the toilet and run back to the front of the train station. It's been twenty minutes now. I turn the corner to where the woman should be standing with my bike box. There she is, standing by my box with the same friendly face in which she first greeted me. I apologise for taking so long and she tells me it was no problem and that she understands my situation.

I am so thankful for her. Over the next months I am to learn that this is just the beginning of the help I receive from kind, generous people in achieving my promise and dream.

First Kilometres in Europe

    I put the wheels and panniers on my Bianchi bike, attached my sleeping bag and pad on the back with a bungee cord and rolled by first meters on Dutch soil. I have my detailed Michelin maps in a plastic cover on my handlebar bag folded to Amsterdam. I decided for the first day to cycle a short distance out of Amsterdam to a campground.
    From the very start I have a feeling of amazement. I constantly have the feeling of wanting to pinch myself to make sure this is real. I see the canals and old buildings of Amsterdam and feel like I have landed on another planet. I forget my map and my destination to the campground and wander in and out of the city streets and alleys mesmerised by all the new sights. The cycling is so wonderful also, there are bike paths along every road and there are many cyclists, most on upright bikes with baskets

on the front. They ring their bike bells as they pass.

I forget about time and cycle and frequently stop to see all the new sights. I love to hear the Dutch language spoken all around me. It is so lively and friendly sounding. Evening approaches and I realise I'm not sure where I'm staying for the night. This will be my first night on foreign soil besides the few nights I'd spent on family trips in Mexico and Canada.

I look at my map for the way to the nearest camping site and with help from the friendly people on the streets I make it to my first European campground just outside of Amsterdam. I pay a small fee at the entrance and walk my bike into a campground unlike any we have on the west coast in Oregon and Washington.

I am used to campgrounds where everyone has their own individual, private space. Here, there is a large grass area where tents are set up side by side. There is another area where campers and caravans are parked side by side.

    I walk over to a grass area on a hill and set up my light blue, quarter dome tent next to the many others. I sit on my foam pad to write my first journal entry in Europe. The doves coo in the trees above. Their message to me is a welcome and a congratulations that I finally arrived.

May 10, 1988
George at the beginning of his tour in the tulip fields outside of Amsterdam.

Discovery of the Friendly and Beautiful Dutch

    My first night I dream that I am back in Seattle at my paper distribution job. I wake in the dark to figure out where I am. I reach out and touch the nylon sides of my tent. I'm not in Seattle. I'm in my tent. I'm in Amsterdam! I'm so excited I can't get back to sleep. At five a.m. I get up and experience the paid showers in the campground facilities. It is the first of many two minute showers.

    I return to take down my tent and pack my gear onto my bike. By 7 a.m. I'm ready to start my first full day of bike touring. I sit to study my maps to pick a route over to the coast west of Amsterdam and hear a "Goedemorgen." Good morning. A nearby camper invites me over for a coffee. In the weeks and months ahead, the hospitality of the Dutch helped me to feel welcome in Europe.

   After the Dutch coffee and friendly conversation I rolled out of the campground. I decided to head to a village on the coast called Zandvoort. The skies are blue and clear. The air is warm. At the camping I was told that this is the first sunny day the Netherlands has experienced in many months.

   Early in the afternoon I arrive in Zandvoort and find a campground in the sand dunes near the beach. I set up my tent and am excited to walk down to the beach and hopefully have my first swim in the Atlantic Ocean.

   I walk the sandy path to the beach and round a corner to my first sight of a European beach. I am stunned and delighted by what I see. The beach is full of people. Many of them are university aged women and they are all topless! All up and down the beach women are rubbing suntan lotion into their breasts. I lived my first 16 years in San Diego, California and grew up seeing many beautiful women on beaches, but not topless women except for the rare occasion my brothers and I would sneak to a nudist beach called Blacks Beach.

I really can't believe my eyes at what I see here in Zandvoort. I try not to stare, but find every excuse to walk up and down the beach.

After a couple of hours on the beach I decided to return to my campsite and plan my route for the next day.

The next morning I started cycling south from Zandvoort. I can't stop thinking about the topless women at the beach. After about an hour of cycling I decided to turn back to last night's campground. I rationalise that it probably won't be a long time until I come to another beach at the Mediterranean Sea.

I spent the rest of the day on the beach at Zandvoort! The weather is still perfect and the beautiful women are still spreading their suntan cream.

When I return to my camp spot I look at my map of Europe and trace my finger on the route I plan to take to Norway. I will need at least five months to cover this distance. Here I am, though, in Zandvoort, and I can't even get started!

The next morning I pack up and start to cycle away from the campground and the beautiful sights on the beach. I feel the strong pull to come back to the beach for another day. It's then that I realise I will never fulfil my promise and my dream if I look back or go back. I decide then on a motto that guides me the whole journey, especially when I come to places I really like. The motto I repeat to myself as I depart is "Don't Look Back."

As I bike away from the beach at Zandvoort I repeat over and over to myself, "Don't Look Back." It wasn't easy.

George's blue Sierra Designs tent, sleeping pad and handlebar bag at a campground in Holland (Now only called the Netherlands.)

The tag required to hang from my tent at the camping near Zandvoort beach.

Bike Problems Begin

Pop snap pop snap. What is that? I look down at my front tire between the two blue medium sized panniers on my front tire. Two spokes broke. I'm on my second day south from Zandvoort, still in the Netherlands. Before I left Skykomish, my mountain home while saving for this journey, a friend working at a bike store taught me how to change spokes on my tires. He said the front tire would be easy, but the back tire would require a vise. He encouraged me to pack plenty of spokes. Thankfully I had about 30 of them.

100 kilometres south of Amsterdam, I easily replaced and trued my spokes. Truing spokes is a process of turning them on each side of the wheel so that the wheel spins smoothly between the brake pads. Within a half hour I was on my way.

The next day underneath me I heard pop snap, pop snap. Another two spokes broke but this time on the back tire. I walked up to a farmer's house and through pointing and miming using a vice, a kind man takes me to his work bench and helps me take the hub off of my back tire to fix the spokes. I give him a dank u well, thank you very much, and am soon back on the road.
    My gloves grip my curved handle bar, my blond hair blows in the wind, and I glide along with my full load of gear balanced between my two legs. My leg muscles pull up and down on the pedals. The open road is my home. I realise I am completely free to cycle wherever my heart desires and as fast or as slow as I desire. I have never felt so free and sing praises to God that I took this risk, this huge step in my life.
    After another two hours of rolling along I hear another pop snap, pop snap. Two more spokes on the back tire break. Ah. This is getting frustrating. I want so badly to just

keep moving forward. Again, I wave down a farmer and he helps me repair my rear wheel. The farmer lifts my bike and grunts. I understand what he is saying through his body language and voice. The load of gear riding on my bike is too heavy. I agree and through broken English he offers for me to leave gear with him for me to pick up before I head back to Seattle.

    I already made efforts to cut weight in my preparations in Seattle. I cut the ends off of tools and handles off of cooking gear. Now, though, it was time to part with items I thought were necessary. I parted with extra shirts and shorts. I parted with two travel guide books. The hardest item I parted with was my Dad's Minolta camera. I'm not too keen on taking a lot of pictures, but I was hoping to take pictures of the people I met on my journey.

    I decided to leave the camera in hopes that people could send pictures to my parent's address in Oregon. I also thought I could collect postcards at places that were meaningful.

    My load definitely felt lighter as I cycled on but there were many times I regretted not having my camera. Between southern Holland and my entrance into Italy, I rarely broke a spoke. The occasional pop snap, pop snap became something I accepted and I got really good at changing spokes and truing tires.

A Belgian Wife?

"Please, take my daughter as your wife," an owner of a pub in Belgium said. After two weeks of pleasant cycling in the Netherlands that included touring fields of tulips, wonderful outdoor markets with tasty Gouda and Maasdammer cheese as well as my favourite sweet treat Stroopwafels, I crossed into Belgium.

I had heard how famous and tasty Belgian beer is and couldn't wait to try it. I was gliding along on the back country roads with green rolling hills surrounding me when I came to my first Belgian village with a pub that had a garden in the back and big open sun umbrellas. I questioned if it was too early to stop for an adult liquid refreshment.

It was early in the afternoon, about 3 p.m., and I still had power to cycle for another couple of hours. I usually cycled until 5 p.m. and knew that a beer would get me all relaxed and out of the mood for cycling more.

    I rolled my bike to the back garden to have a look to see if it was open. Two or three groups of people sat with beers and snacks at their tables. I thought of waiting a couple of hours and cycling on when a beautiful waitress walked out of the pub. She had long brown hair, stunning green eyes, and a figure that was framed in a traditional Bavarian style dress with the laces framing her breasts.

    I was ready for that first Belgian beer. I leaned my bike against a table and sat waiting to order. The beautiful waitress looked over from another table she was serving and smiled at me. My heart beat faster. She walked over to my table. She said hello in English in a beautiful Belgian accent.

    She asked where I was from and wanted to know where I had been and where I was going on my bike. I told her where I had been in the Netherlands but hesitated to tell her I was going much further from her village. I felt a strong attraction to this woman and thought that I would love to have a foreign woman like her for my wife.

The other customers had left and she brought me my second beer and sat down with me. We talked about my life on the west coast of the United States and I asked her about her life in Belgium. The more we talked, and the more sips I had of the incredible Belgian beer, the more I fell in love with her.

She asked if I was alone and I shared that I had left my girlfriend to do this European bike tour. She shared that she was single. I could see myself living in this cozy Belgian village for the rest of my life.

She returned to the pub but asked me to please visit more before I left her village. I finished my second beer and felt the familiar internal struggle. I love women and love being in love with a woman. I could easily see falling in love with this woman. Through my tipsy-ness, though, I knew the reality. I was on a mission of a lifetime. I had already left one woman I was in love with, I couldn't give up my promise to my great grandmother and myself for this beautiful woman in Belgium. Or could I?

I tried to think of the reality that I didn't have a job there or a way to support myself. I also thought of Zandvoort and my motto I developed there, "Don't Look Back."

I decided it was time to get heading to a campground. I needed to stop at the toilet and say goodbye to my beautiful waitress first. I opened the door to the pub and there was my waitress friend standing with a man I was to find out was her father.

He told me that her daughter really liked me and that he wanted me to marry her and take her back to the United States. Holy cows! What?! I asked if he was joking. He wasn't. He said he knew that his daughter liked me and that it was his hope for his daughter to have a husband from the United States.

    I looked at her and she was smiling at me. I tried not to look down at her beautiful breasts. I thought, oh no, here I am, having to decide between a woman and my dreamed of bike tour. I was only two weeks into my journey and I was already confronted with the dilemma I had in Skykomish.

    "Thank you so much for the offer. Your daughter is very beautiful and if I lived here, I surely would want to date her," I found myself saying. I was so proud of myself for saying the right thing, for continuing to be true to myself, for continuing my promise.

    I told the waitress how beautiful and sweet she was and wished her all the best. She wished me the best also. As I cycled away, I coined a new motto for myself on my journey, "Look, but don't fall in love." That wasn't easy to say as I lay alone in my little blue tent that night.

Strength Grows

    I came to cherish sleeping on my 2 cm thick foam mattress on the ground in my little blue tent. After cycling for nearly eight hours and about 100 kilometres each day, it was luxury laying in front of my tent with my head propped on my handlebar bag or inside my tent with my head propped on my pillow formed by stuffing my clothes into a cloth pillow cover.

    Not only did my body gain strength, but also my mind. The years of doubt of whether or not I could live this dream and promise had worn on me and I still had a nagging doubt that maybe I didn't have the strength and courage to cycle through Europe and end up in Norway at the village of my great grandmother. At campgrounds in Belgium and France, people were curious to know where I had been and where I was going.

When I told them I planned to go south through Italy and then north to Norway, I was often told that Europe is not a puzzle and that riding that far was not possible. People often suggested that I cycle some and train some of the journey. I was determined to cycle every meter of the journey to Norway. That was my promise and my desire.

 I earned my bachelor of arts at Whitworth University in Spokane, Washington and spent hours and years reading about the adventures of characters in American and British novels. I often told professors and colleagues that I loved reading about characters and their adventures, but I also wanted my own.

 This bike tour was not only a promise to my great grandmother, but it was also a gift to myself. After 27 years, I finally was living an adventure like I had only read and dreamed about. Breaking free of the expectations I felt as a young man raised in an upper middle class family was extremely difficult.

Even as I gained strength and a sense of adventure, each day I was still nagged by the feeling that I had to have a plan for my future. I wanted to have a solid, confident answer to the question I was often asked throughout my tour, "What do you plan to do with your life?"

I often gave confident answers that usually indicated that I was just taking a few months break from my real life to live this promise and dream. Deep down, though, I knew that I was chopping my former life to shreds just as I chopped my suits to shreds. I was becoming what I wanted to become, not what my father, girlfriends or anyone else wanted me to become.

Now, I want to be an explorer. It was amazing opening my Michelin detailed maps and planning my route for the day on the back roads. I loved the routine of packing up my panniers each morning, rolling my bike out of the campground and sitting on my saddle before most people were even up.

    I clicked into my cleated pedals and rolled away. The road and the unknown continent of Europe ahead of me. Even though I had a route planned out for each day, I often would come to a fork in the road and choose the way I hadn't planned, just because it looked more interesting or led to more beautiful fields and villages.

I often rose at first light to eat breakfast, take down my tent, pack my gear, and be on the road before most fellow campers were even awake. I usually tried to be on the road by 7 a.m.

Discovery of French Attitude

    I cherished my independence and looked forward to discovering where I would set up my tent each evening. My maps had little tents that showed where the campgrounds were. Usually I could independently navigate my way to a campground, but not always.

    One evening in France, south of Paris, I followed the signs for the campground but couldn't find it. I came to a village and asked a young man if he knew where the campground was. He said he did but insisted that I could camp in the backyard of his family house. I thanked him but told him I wanted to camp at the campground. He persisted and insisted I meet his family.

    To be polite, I agreed to follow him. His two story white house was large with a big green backyard lawn. I decided to go ahead and set up my tent. Soon, though, I realised I would not have the privacy I had at a campground. His parents and siblings came out to meet me and wanted to know all about me. After explaining who I was, where I was from, and my current plans, the family invited me in for dinner.

    It felt really strange to be sitting around a dinner table with a family after biking independently the past few weeks. Only a half hour before this dinner I was searching for the campground. The conversation soon turned to how much better French products were than American. They offered me a glass of red wine and proceeded to tell me how horrible American wines were. They presented me with camembert cheese and were shocked when I cut off the white outside which to me tastes like medicine. They gave me a lecture on eating cheese and how French cheese was so much better than the American orange fake cheese.

I wanted nothing more than to run out and pack up my tent and cycle away. Somehow I continued to be polite but soon tried to excuse myself by saying I still had preparations to make on my tent for the night. The family insisted I first sit in the living room to talk more. I then had to listen to how the French language was so much better than English. They made nasal noises imitating English and I had to restrain myself from making jokes about the French nasal noises. After about 10 minutes of insults, I excused myself and went out and zipped myself up in my tent.

    The next morning I got up and packed at first daylight. As the sun rose, I cycled off. I didn't wait to say goodbye. I promised myself not to accept any more offers to camp in someone's yard or stay in someone's house. I didn't keep that promise. I did have some good and bad experiences staying with people.

A couple weeks earlier I did have a positive experience staying at a French couples apartment where I toured Paris for a couple of days while the couple was off to work. The couple were friends of a French couple I stayed with in the countryside two nights before I entered Paris.

Ideally I decided my freedom and independence was too valuable to join myself and my journey to someone else's household and values. At times, though, I made exceptions and learned a lot about the new cultures I traveled through. One time, the exception led to an uncomfortable situation. You will find out more about that later in this story.

The amazing Notre Dame in Paris. I'd never seen a church so long, wide and tall. It is 135 meters long, 48 meters wide and 35 meters tall.

My postcard of the Mona Lisa. In 1988, I was one of only a few people in the room with the Mona Lisa. I got to stand right in front of her. Nowadays I hear the room with the Mona Lisa is always crowded.

I discovered that Lyon is also a beautiful big city in France.

Each day of my three weeks crossing France from top to bottom I discovered interesting cities.

June 7, 1988
The hill city of Les Merveilles de L'Yon.

June 8, 1988

The enchanting city of Semur en Auxois.

Tournon Sur-Rhone
There was a wonderful cycling path along this river.

The remains of the ancient Romans could be seen in most French cities and villages I cycled through.

Disadvantages of Camping in the Wild

There was one appeal to camping for free. It saved me money. I lived on a ten dollars a day budget. A camping place for a tent and bike was usually 2 to 3 dollars a night. The rest of the money I spent on food and a postcard for my collection and one to send home once in a while to my parents in Lake Oswego, Oregon.

My usual evening food cooked over my mini butane stove was a bag of pasta mixed with a chunk of cheese and salami. For lunch I usually had croissants, which, in France, were by far the best in the world. I loved to smother these with Nutella. I often went through a large jar of Nutella each day. It was great quick energy. I also ate a lot of apples. I would eat the core and seeds also. My body craved most forms of food energy.

My evening tradition was to lay in front of my tent eating a 100 gram bar of chocolate after my "tent cooked" meal. This was my favourite treat of the day.

As I cycled south towards the Mediterranean sea, to save money, I sometimes did camp in the wild. These were not my favourite nights. I missed the campground security, toilets, and camaraderie of other campers.

One night I rolled my bike into a grove of trees near the outskirts of Aix-en-Provence, France. I did my usual routine of setting up my tent and laying with my head on my handlebar bag. To keep my mind off the loneliness of camping in the wild, I pulled out my map and planned my route for the next day. I looked for a campground symbol that was about 100 kilometres away. Knowing that I would be at a campground the next night made this night seem bearable.

As soon as it got dark, I crawled into my tent and fell asleep. Sometime during the night I heard the crunching of footsteps in the forest. At first I thought it was probably deer. But these were loud, heavy footsteps. The crunching steps headed toward my tent. I wanted to get away from here but felt trapped in my tent. The steps came right up to my tent. It was either big animals or it was humans. Then the beings started making pig sounds. The sounds were on both sides of my tent. From what I could tell, it was two men trying to scare me. They were doing a good job. After about five minutes of this, the beings crunched back out of the forest.

It was about 4 a.m., too early to be cycling on the dark roads, but I didn't care, I was getting out of this forest. I got out of my tent and stuffed my gear into my panniers as quickly as I could. I rolled my bike out onto the road and started cycling. I didn't have a night light, only a white helmet with reflectors. I hoped this would be enough to help truckers see me. Many times before dawn, trucks came hurling around corners and I would make a dive for the side of the road.

From that moment on, I promised myself I would only camp in the wild if it was completely necessary.

A Long Walk Home

    My original plan was to make a loop through Spain, but, as time went on, I realised the distances were great and I thought that if I was going to make it back up to Norway by September or early October I would need to cut out the Spain part of my journey.
    I got out my complete map of Europe and changed my route. I decided I would go as far south as Florence, Italy and then head north. I followed the beautiful French revere, delighted to be cycling along paths or small roads along the sea.
    I had always heard of St. Tropez, so after setting up my tent at the campground just outside the seaside village, I walked into the port. I was standing by the seaside admiring the views of the sea and the colourful village.

A middle aged couple approached me and asked me where I was from, where I had been, and where I was going. They were a friendly couple and were interested in my journey. After some more friendly conversation, they introduced themselves as the parents of a famous European athlete. They showed me pictures of them with their son. I was truly impressed. Even though I don't follow many sports, I knew this athlete well.

The couple invited me to their villa for some drinks. I thought it would be interesting to see how the rich lived here in St. Tropez and have a break from my simple existence with my bike and tent. I accepted their invitation.

We drove about 10 minutes, or 8 to 10 kilometres to their villa. They promised me they would take me back to my campground whenever I wanted.

We arrived at their seaside villa and sat relaxed on a veranda looking over the sea and continued our conversation about life and my bike tour. I'm not much of a drinker of mixed drinks but politely sipped on a drink they offered me. They continued to drink and we continued to talk. I was getting really tired and decided it was time to head back to my tent to rest my legs. I requested the ride back to my campground.

The couple insisted I stay and visit more with them. I told them I appreciated their hospitality, but that I needed to get back to my campground to rest.

I was expecting them to say they understood and that they would follow through on their promise to drive me back whenever I wanted.

Instead, they took me to the door and sent me on my way.

I stood outside their villa, legs sore from a hard day of cycling, and knew I had a long walk back to my campground. I walked for at least an hour back along the seaside road back to my tent and my foam pad. Each step I could feel my leg muscles not happy with me for straining them more.

    Once there, I laid with my head on my handlebar bag, savouring every bite of my 100 gram chocolate bar, thankful to be back to my simple existence. I had rubbed shoulders with the rich and famous, but was very happy to have my tent and campground as my villa.

My postcard collected at the beautiful Saint - Tropez, France.

A Language Misunderstanding

    Full of a mixture of many good and a few not so good memories from four weeks in France, I crossed the border into Italy. In Italy, instead of doors closing when I entered villages in France, I was greeted with hearty Bon Journos, good morning, from Italian people all along the roadsides. Right away I loved the Italian spirit and returned a reply of Viva Italia, long live Italy! Soon, though, I had a misunderstanding in the language.
    At my first Italian seaside camping, fellow campers passed my tent saying "Ciao" to me. I looked in my small English/Italian vocabulary book and it said that "Ciao" meant goodbye. My heart was broken. Here I thought the Italian people were so friendly. Now I thought they were telling me to go away. I thought that maybe

they didn't like foreigners at their campgrounds.

I finally got up the courage to ask a couple that had just said "Ciao" to me why they wanted me to go. They looked really confused and said they didn't want me to go. I showed them the translation of "Ciao" to goodbye in my vocabulary book. They laughed and explained that "Ciao" can mean hello and goodbye.

Whew! I was greatly relieved. I soon was returning a hearty, heartfelt "Ciao!" to all the people passing my tent.

Introduction to Italian Forwardness

The confusion of culture came at the beach the next day. To celebrate my entry into Italy, I decided to take a day off and relax at the beach for the day. As I came to the beach, sure enough, I was reminded of my experience at topless beaches in the Netherlands. There were many beautiful topless girls everywhere on the beach.

This time, I tried to be a gentleman and tried not to stare. I placed my beach mat, my foam sleeping pad, at a comfortable, non-threatening distance from any topless girl. Tired from weeks of cycling, I laid back and enjoyed being in the sun without having to strain my muscles.

Soon I heard the voices of two young males, probably in their early twenties. They were Italian. They placed their towels right next to an attractive topless woman near me. They started to claw at the sand and make noises that demonstrated they were ready for a close encounter with her. I couldn't believe how forward and aggressive they were being toward this young woman. She ignored them.

    The clawing and groaning went on for at least ten minutes. The two young men then approached me. They asked what was wrong with me. I didn't understand. I told them I was fine. They then asked me if I was gay. I told them that I wasn't and wondered why they asked. They told me that if I was single, I should be laying close to these topless women and letting them know I wanted them.

    I explained that in my culture, in the United States, it was normal to appreciate the beauty of women, but that we also showed respect toward them by giving them space. They couldn't understand. To them, showing respect was directly letting the woman know that they were hot and that you wanted them.

I decided not to argue the point and continued to enjoy my day off on the Italian Mediterranean. The rest, the sea, and the beautiful women were greatly appreciated. The difference in attention given to women was amusing and a little uncomfortable. If I was a woman, I don't think I would like a stranger or a loved one clawing and moaning next to me at the beach.

A Long Interruption to Joy

    Roll one kilometre. Flat. Stop. Unload. Patch. Roll another kilometre. Flat. Stop. Unload. Patch.

    After the beautiful port village of Portofino, I cycled the hilly roads down to the stunning five villages on the Italian Ligurian Sea known as the Cinque Terre. Here, I was in paradise, walking the paths to all five villages. After spending most of the day here, in the late afternoon, I began my cycle out to head for a campground near La Spezia. I hadn't had broken spokes or a flat tire for at least two weeks. Now, though, my tires were done serving my rolling needs. The tread on my second set of tires had worn completely bare. No matter how many times I patched the tubes, something would puncture them again through the bare tires.

It was starting to get dark, so I carried my bike about two to three kilometres back to the beach at the first village of the Cinque Terre, hoping someone there could help me. The village was pretty much closed for the night, so it was obvious I would need to sleep on the beach. I got out my pad and sleeping bag and laid down to sleep hoping no one would notice me and my bike.

Within a half hour a police officer came to me and told me I couldn't sleep on the beach. I tried to explain my situation but he insisted I leave the beach.

I then carried my bike and gear to a bus stop type frame. I leaned against this and tried to sleep. After about an hour, the police officer approached me again and told me I couldn't sleep here.

So, in the dark, I put all my gear on my bike and started to carry it up the road leading out of the Cinque Terre. Even though it was a difficult situation, I was so determined to continue my journey that I was willing to do whatever it took to repair my bike and continue living this dream.

Manarola, Italy
One of the five villages of the Cinque Terre.

As dawn broke, cars started to pass with an occasional passerby stopping to ask if they could help or give me a ride. I didn't want to accept a ride because I didn't want a stage of this journey to be assisted. I felt like if I got a ride, I couldn't say I biked the whole way. So, I continued to carry my fully loaded bike by the crossbar up and down hills for about 33 kilometres (20.5 miles). It took me most of the day.

I arrived at La Spezia, Italy in the evening and tried to find a bike shop. A man in his mid-thirties stopped and asked if he could help me. He told me the bike shops were all closed until tomorrow. I then asked him where there was a campground. He told me about ten kilometres out of the city.

I didn't have the power to walk another ten kilometres with my bike. The man then offered for me to stay at his place until the bike shops opened in the morning. I remembered my promise to not stay in any more homes. I made an exception. To save money to help pay for new tires and because I didn't have power to carry my bike another ten kilometres, I accepted the man's offer.

He told me he was a waiter and first needed to work his night shift. We agreed to meet at the train station at 10 p.m. This meant that I had about four hours to kill. I locked my bike at the train station and went to change clothes there.

While at the urinal, a man looked over at me and said, "Ciao Bello," which means hello beautiful. I recalled the young men being extremely forward with the women at my first Italian beach and figured that Italian gays also had no problem expressing their interest. This was my first clue that this was a fact.

At ten p.m. my waiter helper met me in front of the station. I followed him through the narrow streets of La Spezia carrying my bike fully loaded with my panniers. After about a 15 minute walk we came to his four story apartment building. After applying the security code, we entered the building and I locked my bike at the bottom of the stairs. I unhooked my panniers and carried them up to his apartment.

I couldn't wait to finally rest my body after the strain I had been under the past 24 hours. I only wished I was alone by my tent.

We entered the man's apartment and I told him I needed to use the toilet. He looked at me surprised and told me I needed to take care of my bathroom needs before we came to the apartment. I didn't understand. "What? There isn't a toilet here?" I asked. He said there was, but he didn't want to wake his roommate. I knew then that I made a mistake in accepting this offer of help.

We then entered the living room and there was a mattress on the floor with a large display of pornographic magazines spread across it.

I told the man I wanted to leave. He told me to relax and went to a white clothed table with two glasses of red wine on it. He unbuttoned his shirt and came toward me with a glass of red wine telling me not to worry, that he would take care of me.

I then turned to let myself out of the apartment. The door was locked. I was told I needed a code to unlock it. He didn't want to give me the code.

I couldn't believe I was facing this after all I had been through the last 24 or more hours. I knew I needed to get out of this situation. I first reminded him that he had offered to help me with my bike situation. I then told him that I was not interested in any kind of sex with him. I demanded that he let me out of his apartment. Finally, he let me go. Thankfully I didn't have to use force or get into some kind of fight with him.

At this time it was about 11 p.m. and there I was in the middle of a strange city, stunned at what just happened and more exhausted than I'd ever been. I had no choice but to pick up my disabled bike and do my best to back track our route back to the train station.

Nearby the station were some small hotels. I tried three of them but none of them would accept my traveler's checks. That's all I had left at this time. I had used up my Italian lira in the Cinque Terre.

    Finally, at about 1 a.m., I found a small hotel that would accept my traveler's checks. After locking my bike in their basement I carried my panniers up to my small room and passed out on the bed.

    In the morning I woke up so thankful that I was free from the situation I was in that night. I had never felt so uncomfortable in my life. To begin with, I'm claustrophobic. I hate to be trapped in any small or large space. I felt trapped in the waiter's apartment.

    I'm not homophobic. Even in 1988 I felt respect for everyone's choice of how they express their sexuality and love for others. At that time, I didn't have gay friends, but I did grow up with respect for and a good feeling toward gay people. There was a gay couple that lived behind my relative's house in San Diego, California. These men were always kind and friendly. At an early age, they helped me to see and understand that people are people and love is love no matter what sexual orientation someone has.

　I just didn't like that I was in a situation where someone assumed that I wanted sexual contact with them when I thought there was only a clear message of the desire to help me in a difficult situation.

　I did not wake up with a bad feeling for homosexuals or for any sexual orientation group. I woke up relieved that I escaped from a situation where someone had offered help, but had other ideas and intentions. The waiter, at first, did not respect my feelings and my wishes.

　I realised that I had experienced what many women in the world often face from men.

A Turn for the Better

I found my way to a bike shop and the owner of the shop fixed me up with an excellent set of new rims and tires with the European presta valves. He charged me half price for the new rims, tires and his service. I didn't have another flat tire until the tip top of Denmark. Thankfully, due to this bike shop owner, I left La Spezia with good feelings also.

That afternoon, I cycled along the Mediterranean coast and settled at a nice campground near the sea. Like after my car crash near Skykomish, I once again felt born again after overcoming the hardships of the past two days. I was determined more than ever to continue my journey and finish my promise to my great grandmother.

Two Danish women camped near me that night. I visited with them most of the evening. It felt good to be in the company of the opposite gender.

I wasn't aware of the trauma my encounter with the waiter in La Spezia caused until I phoned my parents in Oregon the next day. I often sent them postcards but this would be my first call since coming to Europe.

After waiting in a long line to make an international call at an Italian post office, I finally got a crackly line through to home. My Mom picked up the phone. When I heard her say "George, George, is that you?!" I started to choke up and cry. My Mom said she would get my Dad. When my Dad got on the phone, through my choked up voice, I tried to explain what happened to me in La Spezia. As I was explaining, the line cut off. I tried to call back many times, but without any success.

I wasn't able to call again for over a week. I didn't like that I left my parents worried about me. I'm sure they had some restless nights worrying about me. I know I would be worried to death if it were my own children calling distressed and I didn't get to finish hearing why and if they were ok.

    My Dad didn't get the full story of what happened in La Spezia until I saw him nearly nine months later. All I know is that he did his best to fill in the gaps to people who asked what had happened.

    I knew he got the facts completely wrong when upon my return to Oregon some friends and family asked if it was true that I had been raped by a man.

The Leaning Tower of Pisa!

My furthest point south near the Mediterranean was the famous city of Pisa. While taking in the wonderful sight of the leaning tower, I met two friendly Danish women who were interested in my journey. I explained to them why I didn't have a camera and asked them if they would take a picture of me and send it to my parents in Oregon. I asked them to also include a photo I took of them. They agreed to, and nine months later when I arrived back at my parents home, there in my mail was the photos of us at Pisa!

On my way back from Norway to the Netherlands, I visited the shorter woman in her home city in Denmark.

George by the famous Leaning Tower of Pisa.

The two nice Danish women who sent our photos to my parents in Oregon.

The Analogy of a Sculpture

From Pisa I cycled over to Florence. My goal here was to see Michelangelo's famous statue The Tribute to David. I found a campground on terraced hills overlooking the city with all its beautiful church domes. Fireflies were my best companions at night at the campground. I sat outside my tent mesmerised by the hundreds of flashing lights of these insects.

To see photos of The David and standing next to it are two different things. The only word that comes to mind to describe it is magnificent. In university I spent a semester creating a bust of a woman out of clay. Michelangelo took three years to create this masterpiece.

I was encouraged by a counsellor in Seattle to see the David and the unfinished human statues on the approach to the

David. In the few counselling sessions I had to help me muster up the courage to live my dream, my counsellor talked about how we are sculpted through life by our experiences and the people we meet. At that point in my life, I was a block of marble just starting to be carved.

    He told me that by setting out to live my dream, I would be starting the harder work, the sculpting, of becoming who I really wanted to become. To see these unfinished statues and the completed David brought home the message my counsellor shared with me.

    I could feel myself changing and growing confidence with each passing day in my journey to Norway. Even though I was filled with doubts about what I would do after this journey, I knew I was being changed and moulded to be someone more true to what our creator had intended for me.

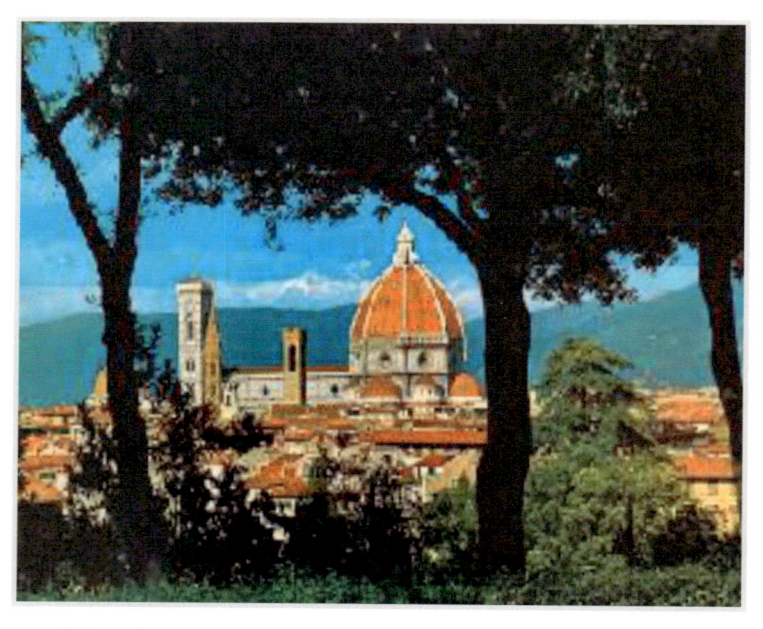

The breathtaking city of Florence, Italy
Notice the steep hills in the background. This is where the climb to the Dolomites and the Alps started right away.

Michelangelo's Tribute to David and the unfinished statues at the Galleria dell' Academia in Florence, Italy.

A Symphony of Flashing Lights

Florence was my furthest point south. From here, I headed north toward Norway. It was early July and I wanted to be on the west side of Norway by the end of August or the beginning of September.

So, the journey north started by cycling through the northern part of the beautiful Tuscany region of Italy. I climbed steep and twisting roads out of Florence and for much of the way up to the Alps. The cycling was difficult, but the views of the rolling hills, vast farmland and the charming villages were worth the effort.

My first night out of Florence I could not find a campground, so, using my limited Italian I learned from kind locals I met, I asked a farmer if I could camp in his fields. He agreed to let me camp in the midst of many rolls of hay as high as a tractor.

After setting up my tent and cooking myself a meal of pasta and salami, I leaned against a roll of hay to watch the sunset. The sunset was beautiful, but what was most memorable were the fireflies. After the sunset, with the approaching dark, not just hundreds, but thousands of fireflies put on a show I will never forget. Across all the fields in front of me fireflies flickered their lights in a symphony of glowing wonder. I didn't crawl in my tent that night. I pulled my foam mattress and sleeping bag out under the stars and the blinking firefly lights. I kept my eyes open as long as possible.

I visited the remains of many Roman structures in Italy. In Verona I visited one of the best preserved Roman amphitheaters. Verona is also famous for being the setting of Shakespeare's *Romeo and Juliet*.

July 11th and 12th, 1988, Lago di Garda, Italy

I cycled along this incredible lake on my way to Brenner Pass in the Alps. I loved it so much that I camped on the north end of the lake for two nights.

A Summit Surprise

After some days, I was soon headed up the Brenner pass to cross the Alps from Italy into Austria. I had been anticipating this challenge for many weeks and by studying my maps thought it would take me a couple of days to reach the summit and start my descent down to Innsbruck.

I proceeded to the pass with mixed feelings. On my journey so far I met people who thought what I was doing was fantastic and wished me much success. I also met with people who told me that what I was doing was impossible. I remember one man telling me that Europe was not a puzzle, that it could not all be covered on bicycle.

As I peddled up the Brenner pass, up the winding road into the Alps, I wondered if this was the impossible part. I climbed and climbed but was surprised that I wasn't getting tired. My adrenaline was flowing hard. Still, in the back of my mind I wondered if I would run out of power and have to walk or catch a lift from a car or truck.

After a few hours of climbing, I came to a parking lot with a lot of cars and trucks parked. I figured this was a rest stop on the way to the top of the pass. I looked closely at my map and still saw winding roads. I asked someone resting outside their car how much further to the top of the pass. They smiled and told me this was the top of the pass. I couldn't believe it. I was already at the top of the Brenner pass?

I screamed "Ye Haw!" over and over as I started my glide down the winding roads. It was already towards evening and I cycled up to a village on the Austrian side of the pass called Trins. As I cycled into the village I met a friendly local and his wife who were interested to know where I had been and where I was going.

They invited me to set up my tent in their backyard. I accepted because I could tell they were genuine and nice and because there was not a campground nearby. I also later found out that the man was the head of the forest service in the region.

They fed me a traditional Austrian goulash soup with fresh bread and vegetables for dinner then fresh rolls, ham, and cheese for breakfast. It was the first of my many wonderful nights and experiences in beautiful Austria.

The main highway leading up to the Brenner Pass. I cycled on the old road below the highway.

July 15, 1988

The village of Trins where I spent my first night in Austria.

July 17, 1988

I took a two day break from biking and hiked up to sleep at the Innsbrucker Hutte above Innsbruck, Austria. It wasn't easy hiking such a long way in my cleated cycling shoes. But, I did manage to take the cleats off for the hike.

A Winter Dream Job

The next day I continued my descent toward Innsbruck. Since I was a boy, I had always loved watching ski jumping and was thrilled to see the famous Bergisel ski jump outside of Innsbruck. I also took two days off from cycling and hiked up to a famous hut above Innsbruck called the Innsbrukerhutte.

After this, I continued my journey in Austria following the Inn river towards Salzburg. Being an avid alpine skier, Austria was one of my dream destinations. I felt the pull to cycle up roads along the Inn river that had a ski resort symbol. An idea was brewing in me to see if I could line up a job working at an Austrian ski resort for the coming winter. I had been a lift operator the winter before, but I also had the idea to be a ski instructor. When I came to the city of Worgl, the pull to turn up the road back into the mountains was too strong.

The steep, twisting road led to the Tirolian village in the Wildschönau called Niederau. I've since been back to this village many times and as I drive up the road in a car I marvel that I once rode my fully loaded touring bike up this road.

As I entered Niederau I could see the gondola and other ski lifts. The village also had the look and feel of a small, traditional alpine village I'd always dreamed of visiting and living in. I decided this was the place I would try to get a job in for the coming winter. I also decided I would try straight away for a ski instructor job.

I had no idea where to go to try to line up a job. In front of one of the first houses I came to in the village a man was washing his car. I decided I would ask him if he knew who I could talk to about lining up a job for the coming winter. I asked him if he knew where I could find the director of the ski school. He gave me a smile and with that memorable Austrian/English accent told me he was the director of the ski school! His name was Sepp Shellhorn.

This is Sepp about 15 years after I first met him washing his car in Niederau. I took this photo of him when I brought my wife to Niederau to learn to ski with the Ski School Wildschonau.

It felt so good to have good fortune after experiencing some bad fortune in the past months. I shared with him my experience in the ski industry and in education (at this time I had certification to teach English in middle and high school) and my desire to teach skiing, and if possible, to learn to teach skiing here in this village.

He shared with me that each week during the ski season they had many tour groups from England with beginner skiers. He said he would be happy to hire me as an instructor for the coming season.

I couldn't believe my luck! I promised that I would return for the winter season. We exchanged contact information. My contact information was the address and phone number of my cousins in Norway. He told me to give him a call in mid-September from Norway and he would then set up a work visa for me in Austria.

I cycled on in a daze. I still couldn't believe my luck! I was expecting much difficulty to line up any type of job in an Austrian village, and here it happened with the first person I spoke to! My love affair with Austria continued to blossom.

The city of Worgl where I decided to cycle up to Niederau.

The village of Niederau in the Wildschönau where I met Sepp Shellhorn, the director of the ski school.

A Needed Rest

    As I left Niederau I did look back many times, promising myself that I would be back in a few months. I cycled on through the beautiful valleys of the Tirol. I came to a beautiful, modern campground in Brixin-im-Thale. The setting was my ideal. There was a river running through the campground and there was a 360 degree view of the surrounding mountains.

    So far on this tour, I usually took just one day off a week, with the occasional two days. In this setting, I took three days off. Once I settled down and rested, my body told me it needed a long rest. I lay still as much as possible for three days taking in the scenery and letting my body recover and recharge after the many challenges it had endured the previous months.

Thankfully, this is another place where a fellow camper took a photo of me resting by my tent and sent it to my parent's address in Oregon.

George taking a good long break at the wonderful campground in Brixen-im-Thale, Austria. Notice the map behind me. I loved to study and plan my future route.

Salzburg, Austria

This is one of my favourite European cities and the birthplace of Mozart. Much of the classic film The Sound of Music was filmed in locations around Salzburg also. If you enjoy beer, my favourite beer garden in the world is here at a monastery called St. Augustines.

My family and I come through Salzburg each year on our way to our annual Austrian ski holiday.

From here, on my tour in 1988, I began my journey over to Munich.

Into the Wind and Out of the Barn

Even standing up off my saddle and pedalling as hard as I can, I can barely make any progress and have trouble keeping my bike upright. After exploring one of my now favourite cities, Salzburg, I headed west toward Munich, Germany.

It started as a sunny summer day. About halfway to Munich and in the later afternoon, a storm started coming in over the distant mountains. The wind of this storm was fierce. I tried to continue cycling into it but as strong as I was, I could not.

I turned down a side road with the hope of soon finding shelter. It had started to rain hard also. After about 20 minutes of miserable cycling I came to a crowded pub. I stepped inside and immediately felt unwelcoming eyes on me. I asked if they possibly had a room I could rent for the night and was given a firm "nine" (no).

As bad as the weather was outside, I wasn't going to stick around here. It wasn't nice to be in a place where I wasn't wanted. So, through the blowing wind and rain I continued down this side road. I was desperate to find shelter. For a while I sat under a bus stop. At times like this, feelings of homesickness would come to me. I thought about my family back home enjoying boat rides and water skiing on the lake where we lived. I even started to doubt whether I had done the right thing in living this dream and carrying out this promise. When thoughts like this came the only thing to do was shake them off, get up, and keep going.

Around the next bend there was a farm field with a small red barn in the middle. A man in a tractor was driving away from the barn. I laid down my bike and ran toward him hoping to get permission to pitch my tent in his barn. He drove away faster than I could run.

I walked back to my bike and decided the barn would be my shelter for the night even without permission. I didn't like going into someone's property without permission, but with the wind and the rain, I had no choice. Usually I would stop at a market before setting up camp for the night to buy my pasta, cheese, and salami but this night I would have to survive on the half loaf of bread and one quarter full jar of Nutella I had left over from lunch. I also only had a half bottle of water left.

The barn was small and square, about the size of a bedroom. It was used for storing hay. I didn't want to just sleep on the hay for fear that some rodent or snake may crawl into my sleeping bag. So, I set up my tent. With the wind still blowing and the rain pounding the side of the barn, I crawled into my tent for a fitful sleep. I usually love laying in my tent listening to a good storm, but, since I was somewhere without permission, I didn't feel at ease.

I eventually fell asleep. After any day of cycling my body and mind need a good rest no matter the condition of my camping. At about 3:30 a.m. I woke very quickly and felt a lot of stress. I just had a vivid dream that jolted me to action. I dreamt that the farmer came to the barn and was very angry with me. He took me and my bike gear to the police station. The police were also angry with me in this dream and planned to keep me in a jail cell.

The dream was so real that I took it as a warning. Mostly in the dark, I quickly took my tent apart and stuffed it into its sack. I then quickly attached my panniers to my bike and rolled the barn door open. I then rolled the door shut.

I rolled my bike up a small dirt road from the barn to the main road. There was the first morning light at this time. It was 4 a.m. As I was getting on to my bike, I looked back at the barn. The farmer was there rolling open the barn door.

I cycled away as fast as I could before he looked up to the road. Now, he might always start his day at 4 a.m., but I've worked on farms and the earliest start I've had is at 5 a.m. Thankfully I will never know for sure, but, my feeling is that someone saw me get in that barn and notified the farmer.

I rode away so thankful for my dream and thankful that I didn't dismiss the dream as just that, a dream.

The wind and the rain had stopped and in the early morning light I followed back roads into Munich. By lunchtime I found a nice campground just outside of Munich and then celebrated my freedom and survival of the previous day and night with a delicious Bavarian bratwurst and beer in one of Munich's large parks and at my favourite Munich gardens, the Hofbrauhaus.

Munich with the Alps in the background.

My favourite beer and beer house in Munich

No Bananas

In 1988, the year of this bike tour, Germany was still divided into east and west. I stand at a roadside rest stop on the border between east and west Germany. Off in the distance I see some viewing towers with what I presume to be soldiers at the top. I pull out my usual power snack of bread and Nutella. Today, I decided to eat a couple of bananas with my power snack also.

I peeled my banana and started eating it when I heard someone say, "You know, over there they don't have bananas and you're not allowed to have them."

I didn't believe what these people were telling me. I replied, "What?! They can't have bananas? That's crazy!" The family told me to speak softly because the soldiers in the tower could hear what we were saying.

Being full of confidence and proud of my freedom, I didn't care what these soldiers could hear or what they would think. I started to wave my other banana at the towers and mocked, "Hey! Do you want a banana? You can't have bananas?! You poor people! Here, come have this banana!"

I was aware that in the east they didn't have the freedoms we have in the west, but I thought that restricting what fruit people have access to was ridiculous.

The family smiled at my brazen behaviour and figured I wasn't from Europe. They asked where I was from and wanted to know where I had been and where I was going. Besides sharing that I was heading to Norway, I shared that I had lined up a ski instruction job in Austria for the coming winter.

They were excited to share that they were from a ski resort village in Switzerland called Andermot. They also owned and ran a popular restaurant in the village. They invited me to visit them before I started my job in Austria. I was given their address and told them I would visit them in early December. It was easy to make this commitment because I had always wanted to see Switzerland and because they had a cute daughter about my age.

    Three and a half months later, this family was surprised and happy when I walked through their restaurant doors in Andermot, Switzerland. They prepared a big meal for me and we shared stories from the rest of our travels that summer. Their daughter was very nice and we continued to write to each other for some months.

Germany and Denmark

Even though I was in a hurry to head north to Norway, I still enjoyed the beautiful countryside and villages of Germany and Denmark. Presently, I can't find the postcards I collected in Denmark.

I enjoyed touring this old walled city in the middle of Germany.

Bad Gandersheim, Germany

Germany has many beautiful, small villages like this that are often only a few kilometres apart.

Missed Ferry

Psshhh. The air went quickly out of my back tire. I hadn't had a flat tire since La Spezia, Italy, thousands of kilometres ago. Ahead I saw my ferry to take me over to Scandinavia and the last sections in living my dream and keeping my promise to my great grandma.

From the border with east and west Germany, I made a fairly straight course to the top of Denmark to the port city of Frederikshavn. The cycling in both Germany and Denmark was fantastic. Germany had many quiet back country roads and bike paths and Denmark had wide bike lanes next to each road. Each country had clean, comfortable campgrounds.

The northern Jutland region of Denmark was my favourite. My favorite cities along the eastern coastline on this peninsula were Horsens and Aarhus.

From my last campground in Denmark, I was given the ferry departure times for Goteborg (Gothenburg), Sweden leaving from Frederikshavn. I got up early to get the 9 a.m. ferry. I was probably two kilometres away from the ferry when my back tire went flat.

The back tire always takes a little longer to fix, but I had it repaired and was rolling again in about 15 minutes. I raced to get to the ferry, but, as I got close, I heard the heavy honk of the ferry horn and saw it slowly pull away from the dock.

I pulled up at the ferry office and saw that the next ferry was at 2 p.m. It would be frustrating to wait five hours, but I had no choice. As I was waiting in a park by the ferry terminal, other tourists started to arrive, some in cars, many with backpacks.

As with my usual experience in meeting fellow travellers in Europe, the Dutch were the most friendly. A nice Dutch girl named Winnie stopped to say hello to me and to ask me questions about my journey. Winnie and I spent the next four hours visiting. We then enjoyed the few hour ferry ride over to Sweden together.

   In Gothenburg we both went our separate ways, I visited some friends I met at a campground on the Mediterranean Sea, she met her own friends. She gave me her address in the Netherlands.

   Two months later I worked on a dairy farm in Elst in the Netherlands. Winnie's home city was Arnhem, very close by. We weren't romantically involved. She was a good friend. She visited me and I visited her and she emotionally helped me to keep up my courage to stay in Europe to follow through with my commitment and dream to teach skiing in Austria.

   After eight months away from home and family, I was at times homesick and ready to end this adventure. Winnie helped me to stay in Europe and to go to Austria in December.

If I didn't miss the morning ferry, I would not have met my friend Winnie. This is a lesson I've carried with me the rest of my life. Sometimes when something bad seems to happen in our lives, it often leads to something good that we didn't expect. Be patient though. Wait for it. Sometimes it takes a while for the silver lining to appear. At the time I met Winnie, I didn't know she would be such a good friend and helper in the future.

Gothenburg, Sweden

This was my first Scandinavian city to visit. True to the stereotype, there were beautiful women everywhere.

This is the Swedish seaside village where I decided to turn to the forest and hills to enter Norway.

The Miracle

This is where it ends I thought. This is the "it's not possible" I was told about. I'm out of power. I'm out of food and water. I slump against my bike as it lays in the sand. My map shows I have about 20 to 30 kilometres left to cycle to cross the Norwegian border. The paved road ended. I've carried my bike again for about two or three kilometres through thick rock and sand in the middle of a deep forest. This road to Norway is under construction.

After a wonderful day off with friends in Goteborg, I woke up charged with excitement and power with the realisation I would be cycling into Norway in the next couple of days.

Out of Goteborg I followed the main road along the coast that led to Norway. Before I left Sweden, I decided to go to the beautiful seaside village of Lysekil. From Lysekil I had to decide if I should go back to the main road and stay on it up to the Norwegian border and Oslo or head up into the hills and forests on the back roads that lead to the Norwegian border and eventually Oslo.

I chose the back roads. I camped in Lysekil and left early in the morning with high expectations that this would be the day I entered Norway.

I biked through winding, small back roads all day. Most of the time I was climbing up hills through thick forests. Rarely did I encounter cars. What a special way to enter Norway, I thought. I made a lunch stop and ate most of my bread and Nutella. I drank a lot of water too, leaving half a bottle for the rest of the day, thinking I'd soon be crossing the border and visiting a shop at one of the border towns.

I cycled with full power and excitement. It was evening time and within an hour or two I'd be crossing into Norway.

I'd been on a nice paved road all day. Suddenly, though, the pavement turned to gravel. My touring bike could handle some gravel, but not too much because it didn't have mountain bike traction.

Soon there was too much gravel for my bike and I. After that, the gravel gave way to deep sand and large rocks. This couldn't be real I thought. Surely these horrible road conditions end around the next bend.

I picked up my bike as I had after the Cinque Terre in Italy and carried the full load by the crossbar. Walking in deep sand and rock is hard enough without carrying a fully loaded bike. I trudged around one bend in the road to see that the conditions were the same.

I trudged toward the next bend in the road praying that the paved road would return. It didn't. I trudged on and on around bend after bend but the road was still deep sand and rock.

I drank the last of my water.

I realised I hadn't seen or heard another soul in the last couple of hours. I looked at my map and couldn't fathom heading back the way I came. It took me all day to get this far. I wouldn't be able to get food or drink that evening before stores closed no matter how fast I cycled. I didn't have the power or will to turn around.

In fact, I didn't have the power or will to go either forward or back. I leaned against my bike and felt dizzy and weak. Here it was my day for entering Norway, and I didn't have a clue how I was going to get out of this situation. All I could do was to pray for a miracle. I prayed for a miracle.

Within minutes of my prayer, I heard young voices laughing somewhere out in the forest. I struggled to my feet and wheeled my bike to where I thought I heard the voices.

I came to a clearing in the forest where there was bright sunlight making a green meadow glow. In the meadow were a young boy and a girl dancing, laughing, and singing.

    I approached the two children a little apprehensive. They might be afraid of me since I probably looked very dirty and sweaty. They waved me forward as if they had been expecting me.

    I pointed to the road and my bike. They shook their heads yes in comprehension. Without saying a word, they waved for me to follow them. We came to another clearing and there stood a small cabin. Next to the cabin was a large station wagon with an empty trailer attached.

    The children pointed to the trailer and then to my bike. Then their parents came out of the cabin and after giving me a kind greeting, we laid down my bike and tied it to the trailer.

    Out of the Cinque Terre in Italy I didn't want help. There I could walk on the road with my bike. Here, though, I could not walk anymore in the deep sand and rock with my bike. I had no choice but to accept their help.

The next moment I'm bouncing up and down with my bike on the trailer as we drive up the sandy, rocky road toward the Norwegian border. The children and I wave back and forth to each other as they look out the back window of their car.

After about 20 minutes of this bumpy ride, the paved road returns. I signal that I would like to get off and start riding.

The station wagon pulls over and they all help me untie my bike and set it on the road.

I reach out my hand to shake their hands in great appreciation. They just wave at me, smile, and get back into their station wagon.

I stand stunned as they pull away, the blond little boy and girl waving to me as they disappear.

Yes, I closed my eyes and shook my head. The station wagon and trailer disappeared. I jumped on my bike and rode ahead to see if the road dropped or went around another bend. The road continued straight.

I had prayed for a miracle. Maybe they had just sped away and I had looked down at my bike to get ready to get on. Maybe I was too tired to see what happened to them. Either way, I stood amazed that this had happened to me as I was about to enter Norway, as I was so close to completing the first part of my promise to my great grandmother and to myself.

Through these people, whoever they were, whether angels or ordinary people, a miracle had been given that enabled me to complete the first part of my dream, goal and promise that day.

I soon came to an intersection with a sign pointing to Norway. 12 kilometres. A reserve of power deep in my body kicked in. I was going to cross into Norway this evening.

Thankfully the road was fairly flat. It was through forest and open fields. The kilometres quickly melted away.

Tears streamed down my face as I crossed into Norway.

Fei Deg!

"Fei Deg! (Curse You!)" a young Norwegian boy yelled as he kicked my bike at my last camp ground the night before I biked into the city of Odda, on the west side of Norway, near to where some of my grandma and great grandma's relatives lived.

Since entering Norway I did make it to a market for food and drink that first night after I was miraculously helped. A couple of days later I did make it into Oslo where I had to have the crank at my pedals rebuilt. The bearings had completely worn out.

I cycled across the Hardangervidda, the largest eroded plain in Europe, and the area that separates east and west Norway. Here I experienced all four seasons in one day. One hour I would be in sunshine, the next in rain, the next in sleet and snow.

On this massive, wild plain I saw how people could believe in Trolls with the scraggly alpine shrubs and trees I saw along the roadside. I laughed with delight as herds of sheep blocked my way forward. I cherished each magnificent view I beheld across this vast open plain. I was so thankful for the help, patience, strength, and power I had received to overcome many obstacles to get to this special place in Norway.

As I sat on my sleeping mat, next to my tent, looking over my route for the next day into Odda, a young boy came up to me and started asking me questions in Norwegian. It had been nearly 20 years since I had learned and spoken some Norwegian with my great grandmother and grandmother. I tried to answer the boy as best as I could but he was not satisfied with my answers. This is where he took a good kick at my bike and swore at me.

His parents quickly came over to apologise for their son and started to speak to me in Norwegian. In English I explained to them that I didn't speak very good Norwegian. They said something that I've now heard many times in my travels to Norway, "Why don't you speak Norwegian? You are Norwegian."

I shared with them my history and they were amazed at how I looked completely Norwegian. About five years later on a ski trip to Lillehammer, while on the slopes, I was asked which year of the old guard (the old ski team) I was on. On this same trip I visited my Norwegian cousin Lars. We went to a dance club where a woman got mad at me because I wouldn't speak Norwegian with her. She said she saw me at the club many times. It was my first time ever going to this city and this club.

The parent's apology still did little to appease the little boy's anger at this campground. He scowled at me the rest of the night and the next morning.

    At this campground, in the evening, I called my dad's cousin Sigmund, who lived in Rosendal on the other side of the fjord from Odda, to let him know I would be arriving in Bleie, near Odda, the next day. Sigmund's family name is Bleie and his mother Laura still lived in Bleie.

In Oslo, I visited the amazing Vigelandsparken. Here I saw over 200 sculptures created in stone, bronze and wrought iron by the Norwegian sculptor Gustav Vigeland. Over 600 figures are depicted.

It did rain a lot in Norway, but camping wasn't this wet!

Unwanted Hugs

It was nearly pitch dark. The only light I had was the daylight behind me at the opening of the tunnel and the glimpse of a light the size of a small garage door more than 10 football fields away at the end of the tunnel. The rough stone walls arched like the backs of giant trolls over me. I had to get out of this tunnel as fast as I could. All I had to do was get through and I would finally be visiting the first home of a Norwegian relative in the village of Bleie. The headlights of a big truck entered the tunnel behind me.

To get from Odda to Bleie, I had to go through a long, dark tunnel. Norway has over 1,800 tunnels with some over 10 kilometres (6 miles) in length. Today, the tunnels are well lit and have safety systems for cyclists to warn cars and trucks that a cyclist is in the tunnel. In 1988, at least in the tunnels I encountered, the tunnels were not well lit, did not have safety systems and did not have any room on the side for cyclists.

I also was not prepared to cycle in the dark. With my need to drop weight early in my journey, I left my flashlight with the farmer in the Netherlands. At this moment in the tunnel, I desperately needed my flashlight. To warn drivers of my presence I only had my white helmet with its red reflectors.

I prayed my helmet would give the truck driver knowledge of my presence as she or he rumbled through the tunnel toward me. I knew there wasn't enough room for the truck and me, so before it got too close I dismounted from my bike and hugged the stone wall as tight as I could. As the headlights got closer, I couldn't bare to watch. I had no idea if the driver saw me. So, I closed my eyes and prayed that I wouldn't be smashed. I continued to make myself as much a part of the cold stone wall as I could.

The truck didn't slow down as it whizzed by me. It came very close to me and I got a sick feeling in my stomach. I did not want to experience that again. I thought I want out of this tunnel now!

I focused my sight on the small square of light at the end of the tunnel. I mounted my bike, clicked into my pedals and stood to pedal. I sped through the tunnel faster than I had cycled the whole past four months. There was a time in Italy when a cycling team passed me on their racing bikes and I picked up my pace and kept up with the pack for many kilometres. With the speed I cycled to get out of this tunnel, I would have taken the lead from the leader of the Italian cyclists.

With probably 500 meters to go, I glanced back to see the headlights of another truck coming through the tunnel. I was determined to beat the truck to the end of the tunnel. I pumped my legs even faster and knew it would be a close call to who made it to the end of the tunnel first. Suddenly, a car entered on the other end of the tunnel.

There wasn't room for all three of us in the tunnel. I had to make a quick decision. I either kept pumping as fast as I could to beat the truck behind me or get off my bike and hug the wall again. I was fast, but not as fast as the truck. I quickly clicked out of my pedals and made another dive for the wall, squeezing up to the cold stone again.

With the aid of the light at the end of the tunnel, the trucker must have seen me because she or he slowed down and waited for the oncoming car to pass before she or he passed me.

My heart had stopped beating for a few seconds, but at least I didn't have to close my eyes this time.

I cycled out of the tunnel happy to be alive. Once through, I clicked out of my pedals and looked back at the small light on the other end where I had entered. I knew I wasn't finished with this tunnel. My map showed that the only way over to Rosendal, the end of my journey, was back through this tunnel.

Once back on the open road, I was thrilled to see the steep sides of the fjord, the deep clear sea water, and the blue sky above me scattered with puffy white clouds. The squawking of the seagulls was music to my ears. This bad experience in the tunnel reminded me that the good things in life are even more appreciated when we have made it through the difficult times. I didn't need to be reminded again, though, so I made sure to borrow a flashlight from my relatives in Bleie for my return to Rosendal through the tunnel.

Even with the flashlight, the return was spooky and required more wall hugging.

A True Viking

    She stood outside a small, rock roofed house in Bleie, a village situated on the Sorfjorden (the south fjord) close to Odda on the west side of Norway. I hadn't met her since I was a young boy in Coronado, California. Ragnild Oma was her name and she was the wife of my grandmother's cousin Sten. Sten, was a merchant marine. As a boy, I vividly remember meeting my Norwegian cousins Sten, Ragnild and Sigmund when they came to visit my great grandmother, my grandmother and my father in San Diego, California.
    Sten had since died, but here was Ragnild waiting for my arrival deep in the Hardanger Fjord. She lived in another village in the Hardanger called Oma over an hour away and had been summoned by Sigmund's mother Laura, living in Bleie, to

help her with my arrival. Laura was traveling and would arrive later in the day.

I took off my white plastic helmet and let my long blond hair fall free. "God Dag George. Velkommen! (Good day George. Welcome!)" Ragnild kindly said.

"Tusen Takk (A thousand thanks)," I replied. Sigmund had phoned Laura and Ragnild that I would be arriving that afternoon. Laura's home was the first relative's home on the way to the end of my tour in Rosendal.

Ragnild and my grandmother were definitely related. She had prepared a large tray of lamb chops for me. There were twelve chops to be exact. It was my first home cooked meal since I first crossed into Austria. Nothing beat the taste of Ragnild's cooking. I easily devoured all twelve lamb chops plus the other side dishes she had prepared that included potatoes and vegetables.

Ragnild picked up the phone and called Sigmund in Rosendal. "Vi har en ekte viking her (We have a true Viking here)," she said. I smiled because I knew what she said. I felt honoured by what she said.

Ragnild, in the white top on the right, and Laura, wearing a long dark dress on the left, with Sigmund and Lars, next to Laura, in the Hardanger Fjord. The photo was taken near Oma where Ragnild lived.

The Last Leg

"Excuse me, are you George Benson?" a boy said to me as I cycled past him a kilometre or so out of Rosendal. It felt so good to hear someone speak with familiarity to me in English after so many months on my own.

I spent a couple nights in Bleie where I met for the second time Sigmund's mother Laura. Recently, Laura had spent a year in Coronado, California with my grandmother Olivia after she had fallen and broken her hip. To see her here now in her homeland and own home was very special.

It was amazing to sleep in Laura's beautiful old stone roofed home that many of my ancestors had lived in. It was strange to sleep in a bed again and I remember needing to sleep sideways because my feet jammed up against the tall wooden bed frame.

I marvelled as I walked the steep sides of the fjord above Bleie and took in the views across the sea water to the other side of the fjord.

"Yes, I'm George Benson," I replied in English. "How do you know me?"

"I'm Gaute, Sigmund's son," he explained. "We are waiting for you."

As Gaute ran, I followed him into Rosendal on my bike. As we came around the corner of an arm of land sticking out into the fjord, I got my first view of Rosendal. It was love at first sight. Two tall, green mountains towered over the village. A waterfall descended from the top of one of the mountains all the way down to the village and out to the sea. When still, you could hear the distant sound of the cascading waterfall. Seagulls called as they swooped in from the surrounding sea. Rosendal was the dream finish line to my journey and became the place in the world that I love the most.

Gaute led me to his yellow two level home which sat only about 200 metres from the sea and beside the main hiking trails up to the mountains. The home was built by my dad's cousin Sigmund.

There waiting for me with open arms were Sigmund, his wife Joanna, and their other children Lars and Liv Signe. Lars was about 18 or 19 years old, Gaute was about 15 years old and Liv Signe was about 12 years old. This was the Bleie family. This was the Norwegian family that I would be closely connected with for the rest of my life.

They opened their hearts and their home to me. For dinner we often had fiskeboller (fish balls) in soup and potatoes. I loved the Norwegian tradition of having another meal again later in the evening. A couple of hours before bed, we'd eat delicious waffles with brown goat cheese and strawberry jam and an oatmeal with cinnamon and sugar.

Taking a shower the Norwegian style was new to me. In the bathroom the shower was just part of the room. There was no curtain or sliding door. After a shower, one just used a squidgy type device to slide the water to a drain.

To keep me physically challenged, Lars hiked me up the high and famous peak behind Rosendal called the Meldeschein. To make me informed about the history in Rosendal, Gaute and Liv Signe gave me a tour of the Barony in Rosendal which is a famous manor house built by a Danish king back in the 17th century.

George on the Meldeschein above Rosendal. Now there is a nice trail to the top of the mountain. In 1988, Lars and I made our own way up to the top.

The Completion of My Promise

To complete my promise to my great grandmother, Sigmund and Lars took me out to the remote, wild island, Varoldsoy, where she grew up. From Rosendal, in a flat fishing boat, we bumped over the wide Hardanger sea water for more than an hour to eventually tie up to rocks at the edge of Flogedal, the settlement of my great grandmother's family on Varoldsoy. There were a few pieces of wood left from what had been a dock and we climbed up to the settlement on slippery rocks smoothed by glaciers.

The settlement of Flogedal was wild in that it was completely surrounded by overgrown trees and shrubs on steep green banks. There were no other homes that could be seen on the island. The over 200 meter deep waters of the fjord dropped away just meters from my great grandmother's home. Steep, glacier polished cliffs over 200 meters tall loomed over the narrow piece of green land where the foundation to three structures remained. The nearest village on the mainland, Mundheim, was visible across from Flogedal and was at least an hour's rowboat away for my great grandmother, depending on the weather. I was told she would row over to Mundheim to go to school about every other day. The other days she tended to chores on the island.

    I walked on top of the foundations and got a sense of what life was like for my great grandmother the first 19 years of her life.

    The remote spot could have been one of my last spots I visited on earth too. After stepping down from one of the foundation walls, I reached down to pick up an iron cover to a stove. I heard Lars say, "Freeze and slowly step back." There, coiled up under the stove cover, was a very poisonous snake ready to strike me. I was able to step back before it lashed out at me. I then got a sense of the dangers that lurked here also.

At the homestead of my great grandmother, I gained a deep sense of my roots and a better understanding of who I was. At this remote, wild, natural spot, I understood why in my blood I always feel the need to be close to nature and often enjoy being on my own. This was definitely a place where neighbours wouldn't be knocking on your door to borrow some eggs.

Sigmund and Lars take George to the island Varoldsoy and the settlement called Flogedal where his great grandmother grew up.

George at the remaining foundations of his great grandmother's home at Flogedal on Varoldsoy Island in the Hardanger Fjord. George still has an anxious look on his face because a few moments before the photo he encountered a very poisonous snake.

When we returned to Rosendal, after visiting the homestead of my great grandmother, I had an overwhelming feeling of relief and accomplishment. I had fulfilled my promise to my great grandmother that I would return to Norway and her home for her. I didn't cry, but I felt a deep sense of awe that what was promised as a boy some 20 years ago was now accomplished. I had been living with a deep worry that I would never accomplish my promise and my dream. My worries sank deep in the fjord waters.

The gold lining of the promise to my great grandmother was that the journey had connected me with my Norwegian relatives. Without the journey, I doubt I would ever be so close to them in this lifetime.

A Moment of Fame

Soon after we came back from visiting my great grandmother's island, Lars called the local newspapers to tell them about my journey. Two west side Norway newspapers were interested in my journey and came to interview me.

I was amazed to see myself in two Norwegian newspapers the next day. They said I had cycled over 8,500 kilometres to arrive in Rosendal. I don't know how accurate the kilometre measuring device attached to my front wheel was, but, after four months of cycling with an average of 100 kilometres a day, the total is mathematically close to accurate.

What one of the headlines said in one of the newspapers was much more important to me than how many kilometres I had cycled. The headline says, "Boyhood Dream Realised." This was the truth.

The headline on this story says, "To Norway in search of his roots." Underneath that it says, "He cycled 8,500 kilometers to his relatives in Rosendal."

The title here is "Boyhood Dream Realized." The reporter got the main idea. (Cousin Lars is with me in each photo.)

The Bleie family, 1988, Rosendal, Norway, in traditional costume. From left to right, Lars, Johanna, Liv Signe, Sigmund, and Gaute. Sigmund is my Dad's cousin. His grandmother was sisters with my great grandmother.

Closing

    I had lived my dream and my promise to my great grandmother. I discovered more about who I was and sculpted more of who I was through all the experiences I had and the people I met along the way.
    I found out that having dreams and goals and pursuing them is an important part of living life in a way that is meaningful. I also found out that it is normal and natural to have doubts and fears about one's ability to accomplish dreams and goals. I learned to acknowledge the doubts and fears and to even name them. I also learned to push through the doubts and fears and make real steps towards achieving the dreams and goals. The saying that an accomplished rock climber shared with me, "Feel the fear, but do it anyway," often came to mind as I was preparing to do my bike tour and as I

was biking through Europe to achieve my goal.

I think that it is important for all people to know that living goals and dreams is not always a piece of cake. Achieving dreams and goals does mean overcoming a lot of obstacles that include fear and doubt. One also needs to be ready to deal with disappointments and setbacks.

In the end, though, determination, patience, hard work and a belief that the dream or goal is there for a reason to make life more meaningful, will make the individual move forward to achieving the dream or goal. Don't wait too long to take action. Life is short. Living the dreams and goals builds confidence and fulfills life.

Some people told me I should wait until I retire or until after my children grow up to fulfil this promise to my great grandmother. One, physically I could only cycle where I did and how far I did because I was young. Two, living the dream and accomplishing the goal built strength and the belief in me that I could accomplish other dreams and goals. Three, for me, I knew that I could not settle down and be a good husband, father, and employee until I had lived this dream and promise.

It is also important to know how to live after goals and dreams are accomplished. There is a great high in accomplishing goals and living dreams that can't always be sustained. Yes, one needs to set other goals and pursue other dreams, but one also needs to learn to be at peace in common, everyday life. When I read my journal entries about how I felt after going to the homestead of my great grandmother, I am reminded that I was frustrated and had trouble adjusting to life that did not include cycling every day, camping every night, and being driven toward my goal of coming to Norway.

I eventually had to learn to find a balance between being physically active and being a social human that could sit still and be in the present with the other humans in my life. I had to learn to be happy with washing dishes, taking out the trash, and helping to rake the leaves in the yard. I learned to not only have big goals, but also small goals that would help to improve life for me and the other humans in my life.

There is a time in life to be selfish, and to pursue your own individual goals and dreams. That time for me was in my mid to late twenties. It was easier and necessary for me to accomplish my Norwegian dream on my own.

With age, I have learned, though, that most of life is about working together to make goals and dreams with others, especially with the loved ones in life. Sometimes this requires taking turns in pursuing goals and dreams and supporting the loved one to achieve his or her dreams and goals.

Other times this means working together to find satisfaction in accomplishing simple, common, every day goals like keeping the house clean or saving for a holiday. The everyday, common goals are important also in living a meaningful life.

May these words and this true story help and encourage you as you move forward to accomplishing your dreams and goals.

Afterward

After the completion of my bike tour I went over to pick apples and pears for a farmer in Bleie for a couple of weeks. I then bid farewell to my Norwegian relatives and headed back to the Netherlands to pick up the gear I had left with the farmer.

It was either hop on a plane back to Seattle or find work in the Netherlands before my ski instruction job in Austria. I cycled some back roads near a village called Elst. I decided to make something happen. I rode up to a farm and asked if they had work for me. The farmer was retiring but told me the farmer next store could probably use my help. He was right. It was the wonderful Van Ooyen family. I worked on their farm for about six weeks before I caught a ride with a truck driver down to Switzerland.

I did have incredible experiences teaching skiing in Austria. Sepp Shellhorn became my guru in helping me learn how to really ski and teach. I've since returned to this village, Niederau, many times on my own and with my Polish wife and our two daughters to ski and to hike in the summers. My wife learned to ski in the ski school in Niederau.

I returned to Seattle at the end of April, 1988, almost exactly one year since I started my journey. My loving mother and father met me at the airport in Seattle and we drove back to Lake Oswego, Oregon. My mother and father were thankful to have me back and proud of my accomplishments. My father framed photos in his office of me with his cousin Sigmund and with me at the homestead of his grandmother.

My father supported me in pursuing the direction I wanted for my life after returning. He helped me to secure a ski teaching position in Vail, Colorado. He gave me full support and encouragement when I decided I wanted to pursue teaching environmental education and my elementary education certification.

After living this dream, my journeys and pursuits of other dreams and goals continued, but those are other stories.

Presently, 36 years after first arriving in Rosendal, I am living in Warsaw, Poland and looking forward to returning to Rosendal this summer of 2023 with my Polish wife and our two daughters. My oldest daughter is named after my Norwegian great grandmother. This will be their first trip to Norway and their first time meeting their Norwegian cousins in person. Lars, Gaute and Liv Signe all have families of their own and many of their children are the same ages as my children. I am excited for them to meet their cousins and establish relationships that keep the connection going with their Norwegian relatives.

I am also excited for them to experience the beauty and nature of the home of their ancestors, Norway.

I was last in Norway fifteen years ago for Sigmund and Joanna's 40th wedding anniversary. Each time I see the west side of Norway, deep in my soul I feel like I have arrived home. Nelsina Brekke didn't get to see her home again after she left at the age of 19. I'm thankful I shared part of her lifetime and that she inspired me to return to her and our home.

I'm also living and experiencing some of my great grandmother's feelings as an immigrant. I have now lived in Poland for 22 years with my Polish wife and our two daughters. My life is very enriched by living in a different culture. Poland is an amazing country with a wide variety of delicious food and places to visit.

But, like my great grandmother, I often miss my homeland and my family. Thankfully, it is easier for me to return than it was for my great grandmother due to the ease of international travel. It is also easier for me to stay in touch with the amazing face to face communication platforms available.

Nothing, though, replaces being together face to face with family. Living so far away makes it impossible to be present for most family events and gatherings. These are a big part of life, and I miss them. As I get older, I make more and more of an effort to reach out to my mother, my two brothers and three sisters and my 16 nieces and nephews to let them know how much I love them.

I have come to accept that in a mixed nationality family, one of the partners has to make a sacrifice. Only one person can live in his or her own country. It is not possible to live in both countries. I can, though, participate in many important parts of my culture. This is made possible by the variety of USA cultural celebrations at the place of my employment, the American School of Warsaw. For this school, I am very grateful.

I am blessed to have two countries and cultures to love and embrace in which I live or have lived, Poland and the United States of America.

George above the village of Bleie in the Sorfjorden in western Norway where he first arrived at Laura's home and where he picked apples and pears for two weeks.

George with Arno Van Ooyen at his dairy farm in Elst, Netherlands.

George, middle in red sweater, teaches skiing to a group of beginning English and Dutch students in Niederau, Austria. He lined up this job while cycling through the village in early July. He had the same group from Sunday to Thursday or Friday. After one day's rest, he started with a new group of beginners each Sunday. He always got his students to the top of the mountain by the end of the week.

At the beginning of April, 1989, near the end of the ski season, Arno from the farm in Elst, blue jacket left, and cousin Lars, white jacket middle, visit George in Niederau. On one of George's days off, they went spring skiing together. It was Arno and Lars' first time in Austria and Arno's first time skiing.

Back Home

George back home in Lake Oswego, Oregon with his parents after his journey to Europe. After returning, he continued to teach skiing in Vail, Colorado and at Mt. Bachelor in Bend, Oregon.

In the off season he traveled, helped build homes and barns, and taught environmental education for the Beaverton School District in the Portland, Oregon area.

He then earned a masters in teaching in elementary education and taught elementary school in La Pine, Oregon and in Jakarta, Indonesia.

He now happily lives in Warsaw, Poland with his Polish wife, two daughters, and two Chihuahuas. He just finished his twenty-second year teaching elementary school at the American School of Warsaw.

He's thankful to all the people he has met in his lifetime. Each person has contributed greatly to who he is. He has learned that experiences and pursuing dreams and goals are an important part of developing who we are, but that the most important thing is to love all people and to be kind and caring to all living things.

My Norwegian Great Grandmother Nelsina Brekke/Olson

The following photo was taken in Coronado, California, USA in about 1964. At this time we knew her as Great Grandma Nacklin. After her death, my father researched our Norwegian roots by visiting the remote area of Montana near Helena where she homesteaded with her husband she met on the boat journey to America. He found out that Nacklin was the name of a farmer in Illinois she and her husband worked for when they first arrived in the United States. After interviewing other descendants of Norwegian immigrants, I found out that many immigrants took the last name of the people who sponsored them to come into the country, especially if they had a common name like Olson.

George with Great Grandmother

I'm the little one in the light blue suit. These are my brothers and sisters. One younger sister is missing from this photo.

In 1906, at the age of 19, Nelsina Brekke left her home and family in the Hardanger Fjord on the west side of Norway. She greatly missed her homeland but never made it back. This is a story about her great grandson trying to live a promise he made to her to return to Norway for her, by bicycle. In the process, he found himself.

Made in United States
Cleveland, OH
29 January 2025